Sweetcake

& THE OLD LADY WHO LIVES IN THE BARN

by Claudie Rhodes

COMAN & ASSOCIATES | *Tulsa, Oklahoma*

Published by
Coman & Associates
Tulsa, Oklahoma
Email: info@comancreative.com

ISBN: 978-1-891116-28-5

Manufactured in the United States of America

DEDICATION

I would like to dedicate
this children's book to my
grandmother who emigrated
from Lithuania to come to
America. And to my mother
who guided me through life
and nurtured my love for
animals. These strong women
taught me how to survive in
rural Oklahoma shortly after
the Great Depression through
the thriftiness we all had to
practice through the very war
years of World War II.

FOREWORD

We are delighted to see Claudie put this story together. What she leaves out is how she has influenced and helped out so many PEOPLE in her life, including the small children she has taken care of and made their lives better. Everyone who has ever met her has come out of the experience a better person.

We never had to worry about leaving her in charge; she talked to our grandchildren about "stuff" they could not talk to anyone else about and she is faithful and loyal to everyone she knows.

We hope all you children who receive this book pass the story on to others and be the best influence to everyone you know. Just like Claudie does! Always remember Claudie and Otis and how they get to know a very sweet and frisky mini horse along the way.

— Trudy & Tommy Williams

Meet Aunt Claudie and Friends

Otis the Pug Dog

I'm Claudie and this book is about me and a miniature horse named Sweetcake. But before I tell you about that, I want you to meet Otis, a warm and loving pug dog belonging to Trudy and Tommy Williams. Not long after I met Otis, I realized that he loved me as much as I loved him. Soon I became a housesitter for Trudy and Tommy while they traveled.

It was a very good match. When I stayed with Otis, he would look at me with a wrinkled brow as if he was thinking; "What on earth is she doing now?" Once I fell in the middle of an ice-covered street and saw an astonished look on his face. I began laughing so hard I could hardly bring myself to my feet.

After a few months, Trudy called to tell me about some miniature horses that she and Tommy wanted to buy. They had found five acres with a barn and planned to build me an apartment above the barn. Our first animals were three mini mares named Sherri, Juli and Sweetcake, a Chesapeake Bay Retriever named Duchess, and a small yellow kitten named Milo. We were the original residents of the barn. Otis stayed in the main house but visited my apartment every day.

LIFE AT THE BARN

We all enjoyed the serenity of country living. I loved being outside and working with all the animals. Duchess learned to give Milo a kiss by putting her whole mouth over the kitten's head. Milo would lie down in an area behind the barn as the horses would exit the barn door in the morning after their honey oats. The horses would stop and give her a big juicy lick which she seemed to enjoy. If I took the dogs for a walk, the cat would follow until she found a friendly front porch along the street where we walked and patiently waited for our return so she could join us to return home.

BECOMING AUNTIE

Otis was a very smart little fellow and when Trudy talked to Otis about me, she always called me "Aunt Claudie." That is how I became "Auntie" to all the animals.

Otis always remembered "Aunt Claudie" kept some of his special treats in the apartment. He loved treats but petting and attention were what always put a big smile on his face and sent his spiral tail wagging. I soon decided to keep a diary of my adventures with Otis and this, dear children, is how a pug dog led to a book about a very cute, frisky mini horse named Sweetcake.

T&T stables, the residence of the Old Lady
and all the animals who lived on the ranch.

THIS IS SWEETCAKE

SWEETCAKE is a miniature horse. Her ancestors were specially bred small horses for the purpose of entertaining the children of royal families in Europe. The country where they originated was very, very cold in the winter, so the horses' coats grew thick and furry to keep them warm. Since summers in Oklahoma are very warm, we shear the horses' coats short in early spring to help keep them cool. Sweetcake is called a Bay Mare because she is a girl and wears a reddish-brown coat with black mane, tail, and hooves.

The Main House

32"

24"

12"

She is also considered very small, standing 32 inches tall and just a little plump. That is because she spends most of each day eating honey oats, grass and hay. She also LOVES apples and carrots which she often gets for special treats at birthday parties.

Sweetcake lived at T&T Stables, a small farm in Bixby, Oklahoma where birthday parties for small children were the main function.

When there were birthday parties the horses' manes are braided with pretty ribbons and sometimes, they are even given party hats to wear. The children get to lead, brush, pet and feed Sweetcake and her friends. All the tiny horses are very gentle and love to play with the little children. Whenever possible, the kids go for rides in a replica of an old buggy pulled by one of the small horses.

Tommy taking a child for a ride in the buggy

An afternoon birthday party at the ranch

Debutante, one of Sweetcake's dear friends

There is also an old woman who lives in the barn! All of the animals knew the old woman as "Auntie." Auntie lives in rooms above the barn, which is the way people who farmed have lived for many lifetimes. Auntie is happy to live in her very lovely apartment upstairs from the stalls.

Of course, Auntie isn't really the miniature horse's aunt since people can't be related to animals. Yet, Auntie knows and loves each and every animal at the stables as if they were her children. Those dear horses love her, too. What do the mini horses love most of all about Auntie? She is the person who feeds them their Honey oats for breakfast in the morning.

Auntie's job is to take good care of the mini horses. She gets up bright and early each day to the loud sounds of the mini horses banging on the barn door with their strong hooves. The horses are hungry for their honey oats... NOW! Each mini stall has one of the horse's names on it. Auntie fills each trough in the stables with honey oats. Next, Auntie very carefully opens the back door of the barn, which opens out into the barnyard, to let all the miniature horses inside to eat. The little horses are all very hungry after a good night's sleep in the pasture, and Sweetcake wants to be the first horse to get her honey oats. That is true of the other horses, too. So, they all try to push their way through the door at the same time, in a rush. Banging on the barn door is a trick Sweetcake sometimes uses in the middle of the day to try getting more of those tasty honey oats.

"OUCH!," Auntie exclaimed as Sweetcake stepped hard on her foot, pushing her way through the barn door, 'Goodness gracious, Sweetcake! Stop being pushy and get into your own stall. Get out of Sheba's stall and stop eating her oats!"

Just then Sherri pushed her nose through the door. The old woman ran to grab the door, catching her finger in it as she pushed it shut. "OUCH!" Auntie shouted again, "you girls just won't behave! You sure are a rowdy bunch this morning! You can't possibly be so hungry with all that nice green grass to eat in the pasture."

As she limped and rubbed on her sore hand, Auntie was able to put the other horses into their stalls. She sighed with relief because each horse was finally in her own stall, happily munching up every last breakfast oat.

Sweetcake banged her trough loudly with her nose to let the old woman know her trough was empty. She stretched her neck over the edge of the stall to see if she could steal Sunshine's oats.

"Shucks! My neck isn't long enough! No more oats there for me . . . Oh, poor me!" She thought.

Sweetcake cringed, "Is Auntie coming to me with that brush and comb? Doesn't she know the tangles in my tail hurt when she runs the comb through them?"

Sweetcake leaned from one side to the other the whole time the old woman was brushing her tail and mane. "Geeze," Sweetcake muttered," I wish Auntie wouldn't comb out my forelock.

Combing makes my bangs hang over my eyes. If Auntie would leave my locks alone, all kinked up in tangles, I would be able to see better!"

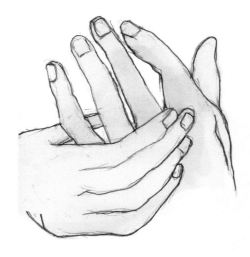

As the old woman reached over the edge of the stall to brush down the back of her mane, Sweecake nipped the back of Auntie's arm with her teeth. "Ouch for goodness sake! Sweetcake, you won't get any oats tomorrow morning if you don't stop being such a bad girl!" Auntie vowed. Sweetcake pawed the floor again.

"Okay! Okay!" The old woman said impatiently. "You can go out into the pasture, but you had better stay clean and be nice. We are having a birthday party today and you must look very nice for the children."

Then the old woman finished grooming and went about her usual daily chores. She had a little mowing to finish at the far end of the pasture, so she drove the tractor to the pasture gate, opened the gate and got back onto the tractor. Just as she was starting to be seated, Sweetcake galloped toward the open gate. Auntie started flailing her arms shouting, "Sweetcake! Get back, Get ba...."

Sweetcake frolicking in the pasture

It was just no use! The old woman could tell by the ornery expression that Sweetcake was not going to obey. She had already darted through the gate and was kicking up her heels. Sweetcake was loose! . . . and loving it. The old woman was in a panic as she knew about the busy street nearby which would be very dangerous for Sweetcake.

The old woman muttered to herself, "Lordy, Lordy. What will I ever do if she heads for the street? How will I ever catch this frisky horse that is so much faster than I?"

The old woman tried running after Sweetcake and pleading with her to come back into the pasture but the high-spirited mare just threw her head high into the air, kicked up her heels, and ran as fast as she could go! She wasn't about to pay any attention to the old woman because she knew Auntie couldn't catch her. Auntie, sweating, and out of breath, was still trying to coax Sweetcake back into the pasture. Sweetcake was having a great time running through the yard in every direction.

Again, she whizzed by, kicking her heels high into the air, laughing with a "horse-laugh" at the old woman. Auntie was really getting tired, hot and angry by now. She had to think of something fast before Sweetcake headed toward the busy street. She would be running over all the flowers in the yard and breaking the limbs off of all the shrubs. Sweetcake was leaving her little hoof prints all over the beautiful green lawn!

"I know just the thing!" Auntie thought to herself and headed toward the barn.

Soon she came out of the barn carrying the "red bucket" which, of course, looked very familiar to Sweetcake. It was because Sweetcake knew the old woman would put those yummy honey oats into that red bucket and pour them into each trough every morning.

Auntie tapped on the side of the bucket to make sure she had Sweetcake's undivided attention.

"Just a couple more dashes around the yard," Sweetcake thought to herself as she breathed in the cool morning air and flung her heels up toward the sky.

By now, Auntie was getting close enough in range to the renegade horse that Sweetcake got a big whiff of the honey oats in the red bucket. Those honey oats were just about the most scrumptious food on earth to a miniature horse.

Sweetcake turned and calmly walked toward the old woman, who was holding the red bucket at arms' length. Sweetcake shoved her nose into the bucket and took out one big, delightful, yummy, mouthful of honey oats. She felt as if she were in horse-heaven! Those oats tasted even better than the ones for breakfast! Maybe that was because she had been running so hard.

Sweetcake followed Auntie into the barn and out the back door into the pasture. She didn't care where she was going as she was completely lost in the tasteful bliss of those honey oats. She would follow that red bucket anywhere as long as it had a single oat left in it. Of course, as soon as Auntie had Sweetcake safely back into the pasture and the barn door locked, she put away the red bucket and the remaining honey oats.

Erica, another one of
Sweetcake's good friends

That afternoon Sweetcake knew she had to be on her best behavior for all the little children. Auntie had already threatened that she would get no honey oats or a special treat of raw carrots at the party if she misbehaved again today. She really, really did like raw carrots, almost as good as honey oats.

Sweetcake was the star of the party that afternoon. She let all the children lead her where ever they wanted her to go. She couldn't have possibly been a better playmate for the children. They didn't have to tug on her lead rope today.

She held her head high and pranced beside them as they walked the horses around the pasture. Sweetcake had a grand time and so did all the boys and girls.

As Auntie leaned forward to help a small boy properly hold the lead rope of another mini horse, Sweetcake gently nuzzled the side of the old woman's face with her big wet nose. Auntie looked deeply into her friend's soft, dark eyes. Sweetcake had been such a naughty little horse this morning, but the old woman understood that is just the way things are. You see, the old woman loved Sweetcake too. At treat time Sweetcake got her share of crispy, crunchy, juicy, raw, carrots just like the rest of the horses. Sweetcake smiled to herself, maybe tomorrow I'll wait and go into breakfast last for my yummy honey oats." Her mouth began to drool as she thought about those delicious oats,... with just the right amount of honey!

The End!

TACK

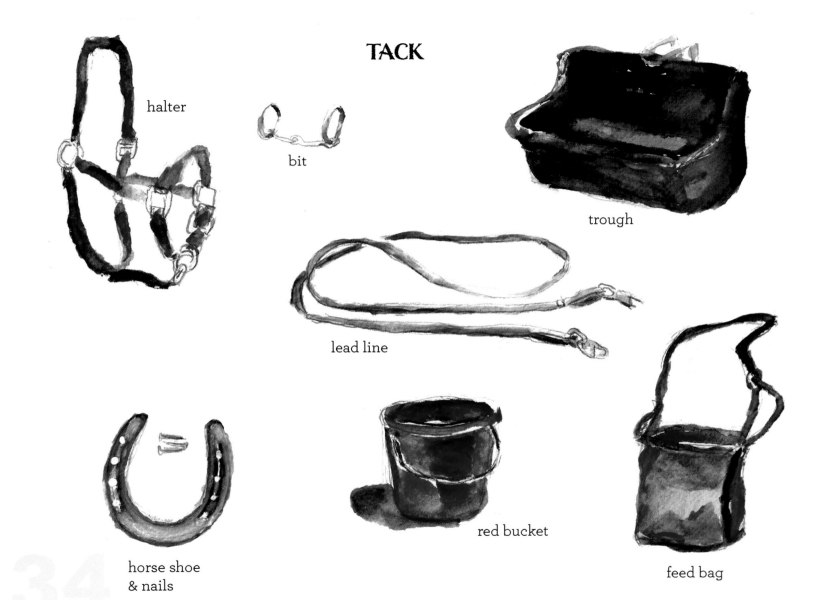

halter

bit

trough

lead line

horse shoe
& nails

red bucket

feed bag

VOCABULARY

FORLOCK – The forelock of a horse is composed of the same material and hair as the mane and tail. The only difference between the mane and forelock is that the forelock grows further forward, sprouting from between the ears. It grows long to protect the horse's eyes from the sun.

HONEY OATS – Honey covered oats similar to the oats people eat and covered with honey like ours are sometimes, but made for livestock and especially horses.

HOOVES – The horn-like covering on the end of a horse's foot — similar to a person's toenail or an eagle's claw.

LEAD – A rope or strap that attaches to the horse's halter or bridle to lead the horse with.

STABLE – A building in which livestock, especially horses, are kept commonly means a building divided into separate stalls where individual animals are kept.

STALLS – a structure in the stable or barn to divide the space for animals such as horses.

TACK – Any equipment and supplies for horses.

TAIL – Hangs at the back of the horse and has the same kind of long, course hair as the mane and forelock. The horse uses its tail to shoo the flies off itself.

TROUGH – A hollowed out structure that animals eat out of.   The word refers to the shape of the container. It is low and hollowed out. Long ago people ate from troughs. Then they became fancy and made individual plates and bowls to eat from. I think we all like this way of eating much better!

buggy

Claudie Rhodes – My Story

A few years before the miniature horses, I became acquainted with Trudy and Tommy Williams. My husband had passed away a little over two years prior and I was working as catering supervisor at the Tulsa County Fairgrounds. After about two and a half years of struggling to work and maintain the property, I took a good look and realized I was fighting a losing battle. As badly as I wanted to stay there in the serenity of country living, I knew I had to do something as I could not let the property get into a state of disrepair. I started taking note of the monthly real estate sales and soon decided that would be the least painful avenue for this old sentimental woman to take. So, I walked into Trudy's real estate office one day, and in a very weak voice said, "I want to auction my home." The experience was handled in such a caring and professional manner that I was as much at ease as one could have been. It turned out to be very successful move on my part. Not only did I sell my house but also became friends with the Williams family.

Sometime later, after I was settled in a smaller home in Tulsa, a few friends and I decided to start a small stock club. I invited Trudy and she decided to host the first meeting in her home. That was my first meeting with Otis, the pug, and it was a mutual love attraction.

Trudy called me one day and asked if I would be interested in house sitting with Otis while they traveled. Otis was so loving and, as I had lost my dog during my husband's illness, he filled a very big void. It was a very good match.

With much encouragement from Trudy and James Gallagher, the book's illustrator, the book about Sweetcake was conceived. I want to thank James for all the hours of labor as we tried to make the book interesting, entertaining and educational for the children. His very talented illustrations, computer knowledge, and above all, his gift of patience with "the old lady who lives in the barn" have contributed much to the book. I also must thank Trudy and Tommy for their many wonderful years of friendship, guidance, and encouragement along the way. They are the type of friends that always will be there for you!

James Gallagher – Illustrator

I have listened for hours to Claudie Rhodes, *Sweetcake's* author, reveal many chapters of her rural upbringing, working life, and worldly experience, in awe of her rare and plainspoken perspective on life. When she told me that she had a children's book she dreamed of publishing, I thought I had a responsibility to share her manuscript with the world.

I am a Fine Artist/Jack of all trades; the kind of person one is likely to cross paths with in Oklahoma or Tulsa.

"As an artist, I have exhibited my art from Tulsa to Taiwan."

As a tradesperson I have restored many older homes for grateful homeowners. That is how I met the author, Claudie Rhodes.

I actually convinced Claudie that with a few of my illustrations there would be nothing to stop her from publishing her first book, *Sweetcake & the Old Woman Who Lives in the Barn*. I hope you enjoyed reading this book and learning from this sage and scholar of the prairie.